poetry

in parts

by resarf poetry

(~)

(& so it doth begineth

it so & hath doth it

so begineth hath it &)

...

obligatory preamble

a wise man once said

save the hodgepodge

cerebral sheep graze

god bless bodge jobs

save the hedgehog

lend us a fiver

black holes are mysteries

scrumpy my cider

reality's oblong

bring back echoes

forget the bloody fire

oh blow the bellows

summer can do soup too

bollocks in motion

i hereby declare

this fucking poem open

...

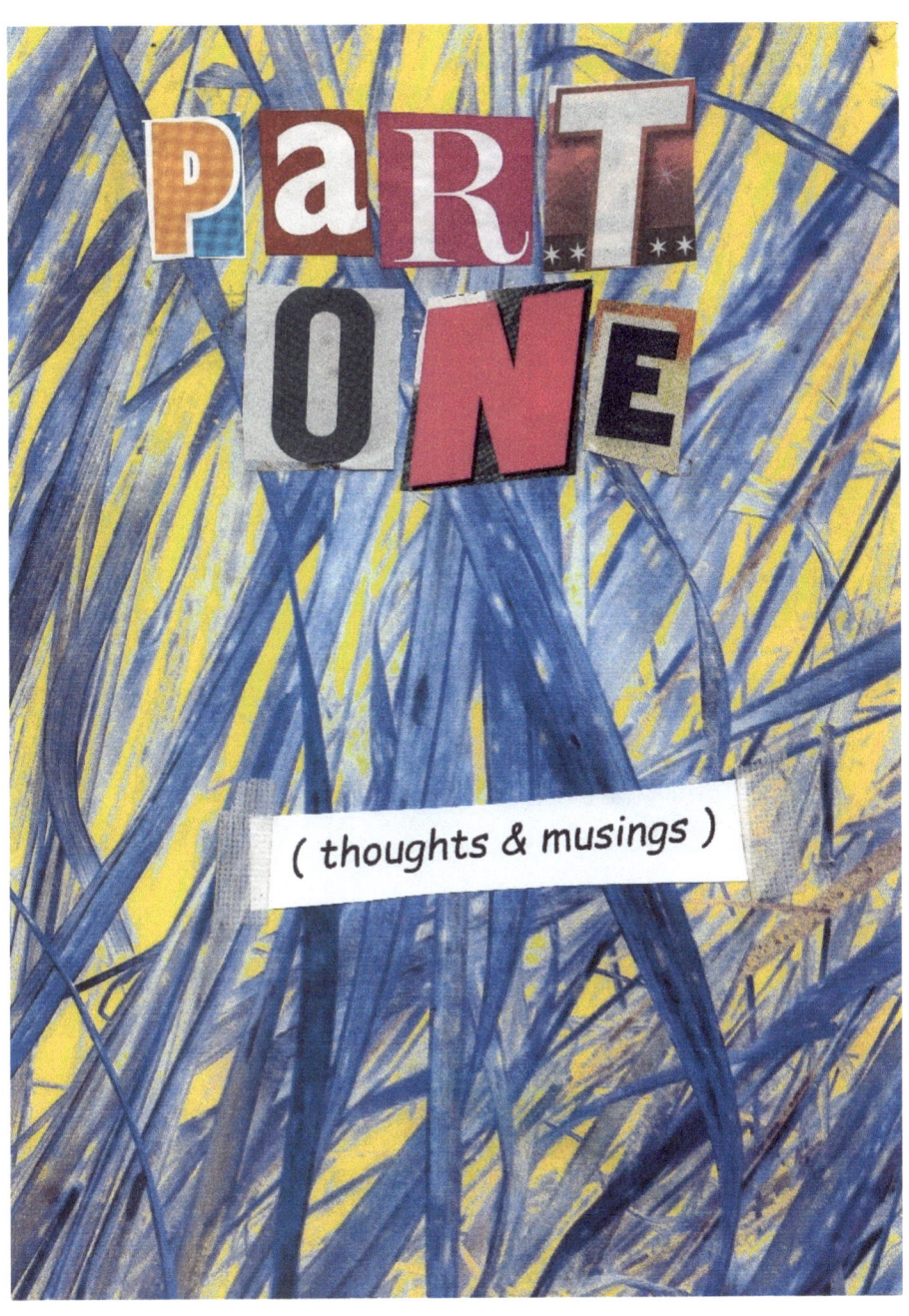

PART ONE

(thoughts & musings)

before backwards

before backwards there was forwards

before sideways

there was straight

before slouching there was upright

before burst

there was inflate

before sliced bread there were bread knives

before chickens

dinosaurs

before t.v there were hangings

before before

there was before

(but that's another story)

...

what is monday?

what is monday? is it real?

how does monday make you feel?

what's its essence? what's its core?

can its magic open doors?

can we pat it on the head?

pretend it's a dog instead?

'good boy monday – please don't bark

giz five minutes then we'll go

down the park'

...

let's go dutch

let's go dutch & split this bill

clogs not reeboks - live in windmills

eat edam cheese til we're ill

at sea level

who needs hills

(?)

cafés, courage, canals - yeah

why we could cycle everywhere

with our uncles - harsh but fair

tulip flowers

in our hair

...

do as those romans are

when in rome

do as those romans are

in a toga ride a vespa

down a backstreet

after dark

worship old popes

or gods named after planets

pick

your roman nose

(?)

(but beware

those ides of march)

...

for the almost

just a quick thought

for the almost

the ones that nearly did it

but dot-dot-dot

like vercingetorix

or captain robert falcon scott

(your efforts have been noted)

...

certainly

i know my hand

like riding a bike

on the back of my hand

as sure as pike

might bite my hand

shit – which little finger?

on an as clear as day

if i stick it in the river

so theres

...

the mystery of soup

soup

the food

that makes us piss

(?)

soup

the drink

that makes us shit

(?)

confusing,

isn't it?

...

percy shaw

he purred not a whisper

nor curled up for naps

but percy shaw saw

with the eyes

of a cat

...

an assortment

another daze - another wobble

sprained is day yet on she hobbles

maelstroms suck

fat turkey's gobbles

puddles muddles

pigeons squabble

oh yonder dales beyond those windmills

with the sound of the bastard hills

resonate

rattle windowsills

turn my biro

into a quill

# of wobbles

save mater earth & keep bees on it

stationary supersonic

shanks's pony

plate tectonic

clubfoot sandwich

language phonics

save the slogan & jellied quibbles

bad shrew jokes - byzantine riddles

piggys in the

midst of middles

dogs called god &

cats called tiddles

...

gibbons

stanley gibbons

swang branch to branch

lived in the jungle

collected stamps

edward gibbon

climbed the trees tall

scratched his ape nuts so

wrote of rome's fall

...

musings on teeth & bees

people with no teeth

& no false teeth

trying to speak

are always a right bastard to understand

it's a bit like if we zapped bees

& made them human size

with human brains like we

because bees don't have teeth

not like us but

they could buzz intelligently

plus with six limbs

they could easily wave semaphore

i would pay too much money to see that

shit loads & that

...

(~)

e

n

d

o

f

p

a

r

t

o

n

e

...

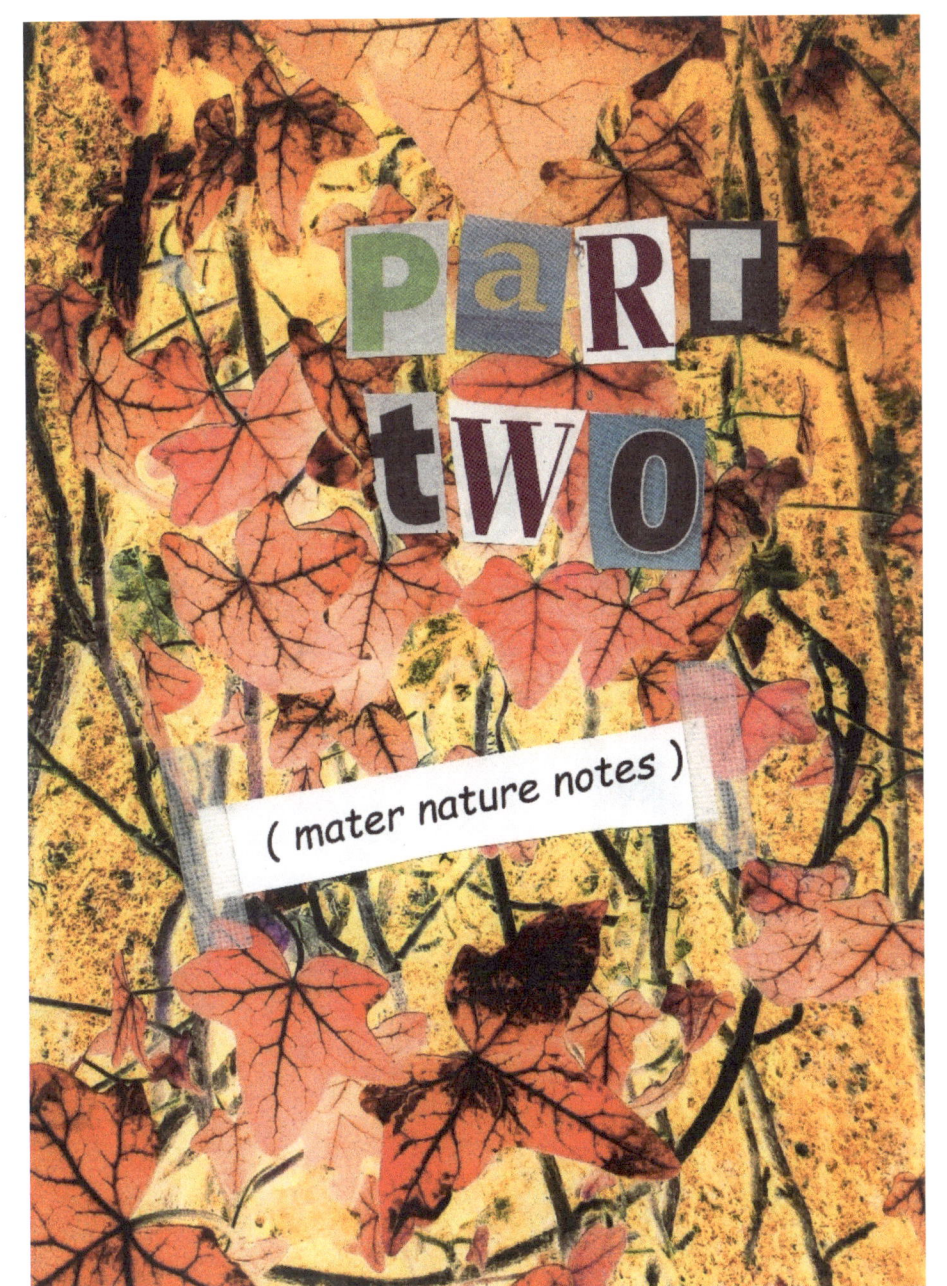

PART TWO

(mater nature notes)

midsummer murmurs

there are echoes in the hedgerows

of the babbles in the brambles

sticky whispers in the thicket

where that goosegrass tangles

as june's a spinning jenny

she's a loom of a loon

halfway up the greasy pole

a strawberry moon

...

good for bobbins

good for bobbins

starts the ogham

among treed folk

plenty of 'em

they're the organ

woods are churches

drink their rich sap

silver birches

...

riverbank job

rob a riverbank

with a bb gun

your money or meanders

then go on the run

(splash the cash)

...

cloud folk portent?

whist gazing up this afternoon

i saw a cloud that looked like you

she had your eyes & sad ears too

also the same **fuck off** tattoo

on her forehead then off she went

then merged into the duke of kent

features clash-smashed, twisted & bent

was this some strange

cloud folk portent

(?)

...

it's the ape (interface)

flabbergasted

cheeky bastards

bloody hazards

it's the ape

~

opto-thermic

part mashed turnip

where's y'permit?

(interface)

...

nearly home now ...

yes i could see my house from here

if all this mist would disappear

if this piss rain would dissipate

if this fog would evaporate

if these glasses were super-strength

if this hilltop - well up it went

just like some magic bean-stalked plant

(down there somewhere's my house of ant)

(?)

...

sniffing gusts

in my mind the northern lights glow

down comes the wind with arctic gusts

its subtle hints of eskimo

& faint whiffs of polar bear musk

so when the wind from the south blows

can they too sense the distant near?

i have quite a sensitive nose

(my nose has froze since standing here)

...

(then)

yet when does winter become spring

(?)

as nutjob snowdrops bloom through snow

(?)

when buds begin their blossoming

(?)

when birds sing so

(they seem to know)

...

nature

yes nature knows

the price of tea

in china like

their steel it's cheap

the saying goes

as followed through

please see above

then back to you

as it's all maths

uncharted maps

the margins &

the paragraphs

confusion reigns

on subject brains

yet kings aint

nature - smudges stain

knows

a wonky smile

of maybes too

zephyrus west

breeze sneeze a clue

there's wicked tricks

& booby traps

so please fill in

the many gaps

thus help us out

is this a quiz?

yes buzz in if

you think it is

with answers please

please some of those

& no cheating

as nature knows

...

thistle season

come july it's spiky

as the mind's slightly fizzled

with a purposeful purple

amid summer's coloured riddles

an 'erb & a flower

tell a friend - blow a whistle

they're nutty on the inside

'tis the time of the thistle

...

mid-cucumber season

mid-cucumber season

is mayhem although

we're asking for madness

when cucumbers grow

the limbo within in

beyond rhyme or reason

the green heart of khaos

mid-cucumber season

...

(~)

e

n

d

o

f

p

a

r

t

t

w

o

...

paRT
Three

(tales from the dales & beyond)

polly left the iron on

polly left the iron on

polly left the iron on

polly left the iron on

her house burned down

...

the man with no toenails but toes

they say he was born on a weekday

the man with no toenails but toes

in the maternity ward

of a hospital

but which one? no one knows

~

in many ways he was shrouded in mystery

which helped the devil-magic rumours thrive

so an angry mob & i bumped him off last tuesday

sleep tight

boiled alive

...

visions of things

i was amble-plodding down a y'oldey wonky lane

to my left a field of donkeys

in the head an empty brain

to my right a field of peas when the visions burst forth

yes pods aplenty

as a jenny eeyored

i saw next ash wednesday it rained around 3ish

a ginormous artichoke

an otter feeling peevish

a baboon in a wedding dress - two pixies playing badminton

& then shite faded out to nowt

- should i inform the vatican

(?)

...

odds, sods 'n' gods

writing notes on scraps of paper

dagon ploughing – see y'later

hathar's waving - oscillator

great stuff like the magna mater

scrawls of sprawl this navigator

cernunnos the radiator

i've stowed away on a freighter

(your dinner's in the oven)

...

the village of keiths (!)

i live in a village

where everyone's keith

every man, woman & child is

called keith

keiths build up like limescale

but a secret i keep

i'm the only non-keith

so i lie

" hi,

i'm keith "

...

beethoven's van

a man with a van

is a man of the van

ludwig van man

beethoven man

man of the van

conducting hands

orchestrate van

man with a van

(ludwig van man)

...

the incredible-flexible poem

the incredible-flexible poem

this poem

is gymnastic

the incredible-flexible poem

octopus-esque

elastic

the incredible-flexible poem

stretchy stretchy

fantastic

the incredible-flexible poem

oh, shittabrick

- i've snapped it

...

longer than expected

he queried the length

of a country mile

so he set out on foot

through field - o'er stile

until he could know

as no figure exists

that was twelve years ago

we've not seen him since

...

night time

night time

not day

bats flap

cats stray

deep sleeps

ash trays

t.v

duvets

chapters

whisky

willows

wispy

jim-jams

frisky

home time

miss me?

not day

night time

moon-based

faster

slow-paced

you choose

two-faced

janus

snails race

slippers

cocoa

clubbers

go-go

seal pups?

oh no

then dawn

(cock crows)

...

the girl with carrots for fingers

the girl with carrots for fingers

had actual carrots for fingers

i met her one crunchy

candlemas eve

hiding in a wood

amidst the frosty old trees

the girl with carrots for fingers

oh how her carrot touch lingers

she escaped from a farm-lab

then lived on the run

a super-hush experiment

& potentially; weapon

yes the girl with carrots for fingers

don't worry - her hair wasn't ginger

we spoke of a future

her voice was a song

but come the yawn of morning-thing

that carrot girl had gone

...

there may be ghost tales ...

up on yon moorland

amid eerie fog

where heather grows so

by y'oldey peat bogs

beyond the tree-line

where cautious owls hoot

there may be ghost tales

& legends to boot

...

(~)

e

n

d

o

f

p

a

r

t

t

h

r

e

e

...

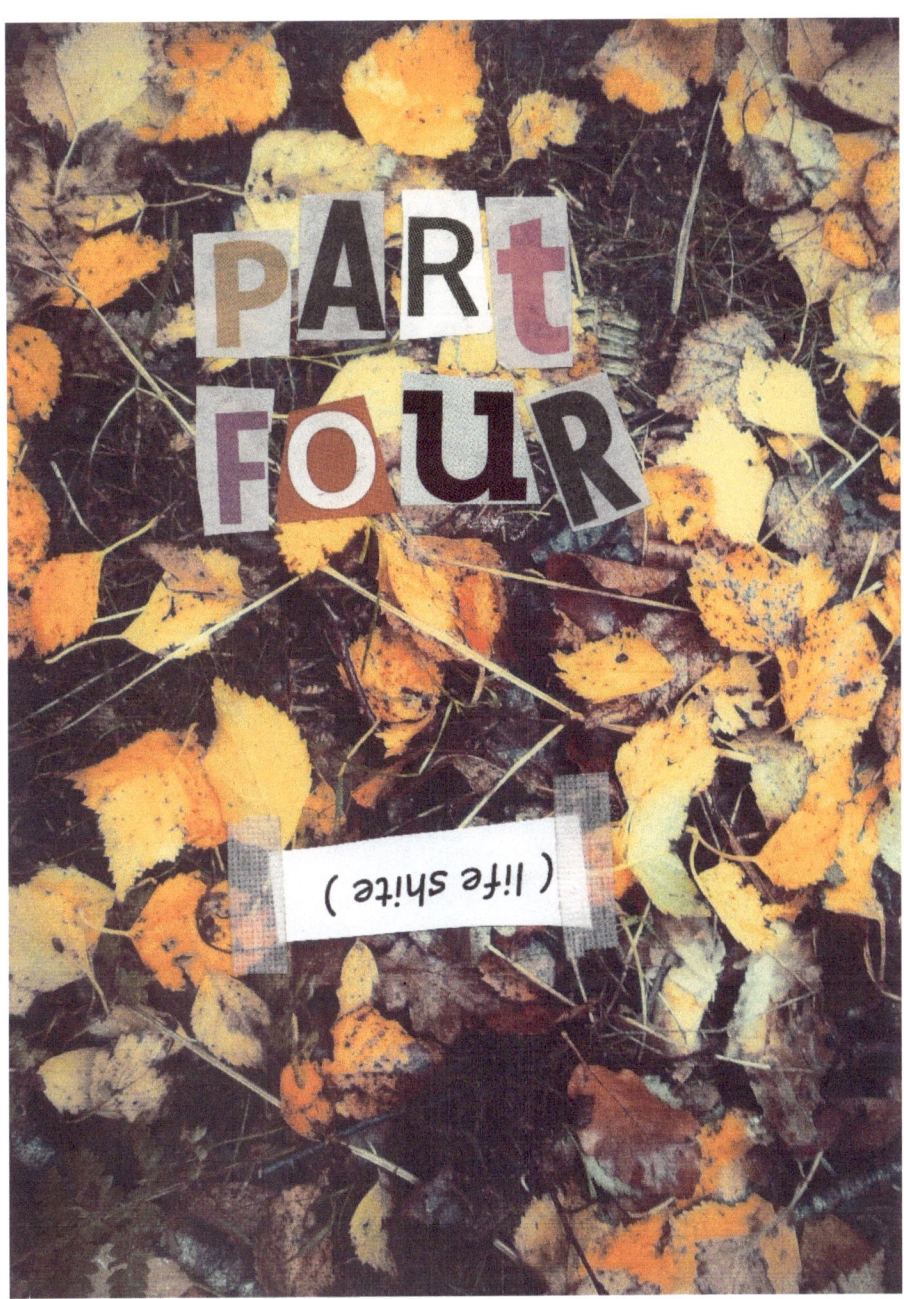

PARt
FOUR

(life shite)

fook thuh skumm

at knight i toss

bee neath my sheets

with nightscarez ov thee

grammar police

thy CAPITALS

& dickshunreez

No, it's dictionaries.

~

aarrghh

help me

please

...

esoteric chaffinches

yes sunday is the otter's egg

the synergy of gathered time

its energy - our scrambled heads

the weathering of battered rhymes

its gravy flowing through our veins

those crumbles in our custard creams

a gentle tap upon our brains

et déjà vu within our dreams

it's esoteric chaffinches

& pretty maids all in a row

all puzzled polecat - laughing fish

it's television comatosed

it's drunken uncles stuck up trees

long strolls along the edge's span

tis one for you - fifteen for me

it's babychamed – diazepamed

...

conversations with florence

i've been chatting

with the statue

of florence

in town

we discussed lamps

the crimea

& owls

the medici

light-winged dryads

her stone lips

unmoved

yet sound

(she's always good

for a natter if

i'm knockin' around)

...

bus station poem

at bay twenty's

human zoo

patience - stations

queues for queues

old folk natter

that & this

odd folk they write

shat like this

un-tinned sardines

waiting for

godot or the

six point four

or the rapture

trumpets blown

(hurry driver)

(help us home)

...

tongue in cheek

there in my mouth

my tongue in cheek

not coventry

or mozambique

the arctic tern

flies to & fro

but tongues are stuck

where can they go

(?)

...

biscuit magic

biscuits

take the ...

taste it

dip it

biscuits

love 'em

lifeblood

live it

biscuits

problem?

risk it

fix it

biscuits

top shit

magic

mystic

...

leaky stuff

yes information leaks from me

maybe within there lurks a mole?

certain key words lie splurged on streets

so find that traitor – block that hole

my journal from last whitsun eve

is soon to be a west end play

that mental note one wrote last week

arrived in the post yesterday

(?)

...

mucking about by the river

mucking about by the river

watching swans just swan along

eiders & the odd kingfisher

(mumbling bit of jumbled songs)

in the sunlight ripples glisten

dazzling my half-arsed eye

calm currents they whisper - listen

(lobbed-in beer cans bob on by)

should i find an empty bottle?

write a note to float inside?

with a quote from aristotle

(a gift for whomever finds)

' hello you, i'm by the river

watching swans just swan along

eiders & the odd kingfisher

(a blue swish & then it's gone) '

...

acrostic

p hantom penguins

pickled plums

peppermint pricks

parsnip puns

o smosis ooze

onion odes

octane occult

overloads

e agle-eyed ears

eclogue elms

electric earls

eggy elves

to bear

t ipsy teapots

tempered twerps

ten thousand tents

tetchy turds

r umplestiltskin

radishes

rhubarb ructions

ravishes

y obbish yeomans

yellowy

yawning yokels

p o e t r y

...

do sphincters speak in riddles?

this blue van is reversing

this man wants compensation

this man wants reimbursing

his shits want constipation

the weir is overflowing

down dale it's pissy drizzle

up in them peaks it's snowing

do sphincters speak in riddles?

of lynxes & of sphynxes

flighty & quite magical

unlucky are jinxed winches

minstrels sing in madrigal

of cranes & jigsawed muddles

as sundries lie in waiting

the many fucking puzzles

as day is just awaking

...

repetition is the key

repetition is the key

repetition is the key

repetition is the key

(that's it)

...

(~)

e

n

d

o

f

p

a

r

t

f

o

u

r

...

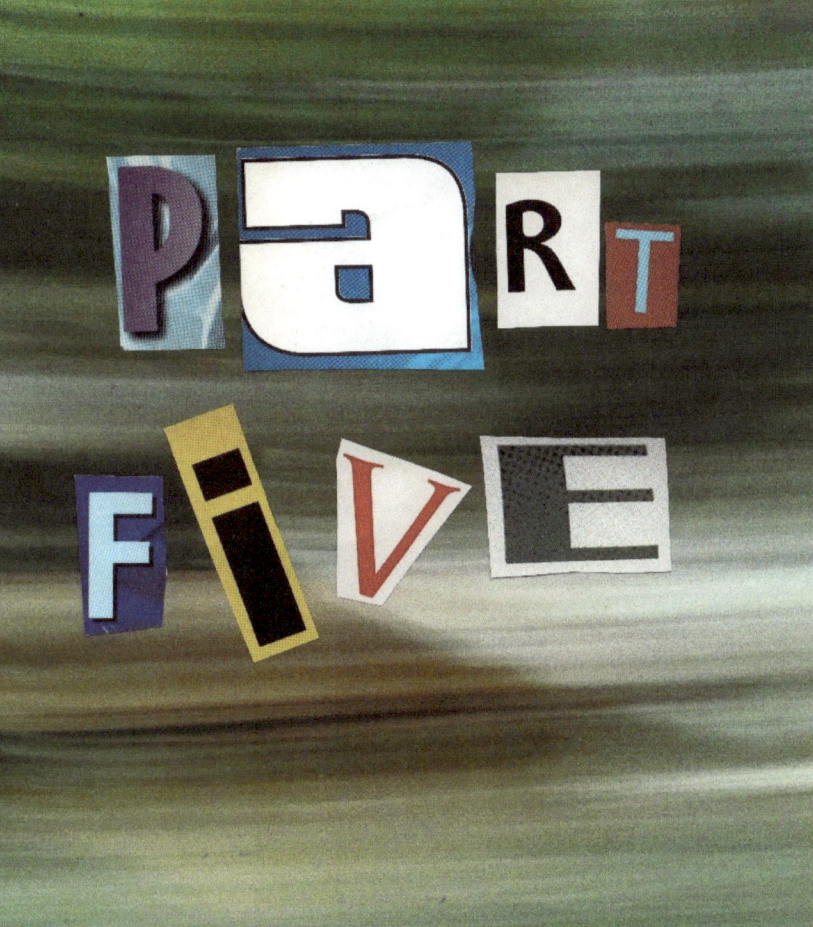

(part five)

my farmer lives

down in ancient sumer there

i herded goats

up in caledonia

i tilled them oats

in the fourteenth century

i tended sheep

when all was victorian

i gathered wheat

before scarecrows came along

i scared the crows

when the vikings invaded

my sows farrowed

with straw in my mouths - with my

rosy cheeked wives

but not in this life

(no)

- in my farmer lives -

...

anyone for cricket?

anyone for cricket?

whites & sticky wickets

the leg-a-rubbing insects

singing in the thicket

please bowl us a googly

as you won't confuse me

if the umpire signals out

i'll flash 'em a moonie

agricultural ducks

lewis method dumb fucks

fruit salad & furniture

on the boundary - bad luck

topspin twenty20

breathless hushes testy

tea in the pavilion

sandwiches aplenty

...

the corduroy years

& so then things wrote of the corduroy years

with fettled head

as blue tits fed

from yon bird feeder as them curtains twitched

with sacheted cups

hot, cheapskate sups

of shite poundland fare - passing sirens blare

another pen

stops working then

then the doorbell rings & a dodo sings

of easters nu

rebooting spring

(already?)

...

monkeys in helicopters

monkeys in helicopters

army ants in army tanks

stoats afloat on norse long boats

& giraffes

in hovercrafts

...

the first poet to time travel

the first poet

to time travel

wrote a wonky sonnet

in ancient rome

briefly called babylon

their muse

& home

then fled

to some dome

on some planet yet

unknown

...

footpath yonder

absence makes the heart grow fonder

essex makes the girl go blonder

madness makes the sane go bonkers

money for jam makes the hansie grow cronje

questions make the nosy ponder

pauses make the days last longer

civics makes the car go honda

footpath yonder

(on one wanders)

...

pine cones

pine cones

rhinos

tough them

mind-zones

pine cones

rhizomes

hi-fi

ozone

cone pines

confines

white noise

red whine

cone pines

home time?

time for home

(mind your own)

...

the month of jan

the month of jan

when things began

snow white rabbits

pinch punch - ow man

perhaps begun?

the head's still spun

the bare bones of

time's skeleton

begin afresh

the same old mess

biscuits - risk it

each step's a guess

still miss 'n' hit

trapdoors 'n' tricks

but early days

(don't shit them bricks)

...

floaty

floaty ghosts

restless

hauntings

momentum

springtime

a crocus

restless

no focus

cheese rolling

multi-plug

cobwebs

delusions

am i florence nightingale?

maybe

confusion

ghosts

are you isaac newton?

momentum

& hauntings

late spring

mid-autumn

potholing is

daunting

from pheasant

to peasant

from pauper

to crown

atishoo

atishoo

we all fall

down

...

as it's not pancake day

as it's not pancake day

nah - not today

no shrovetide / nosedive

no lent on its way

i'll dawdle the edgelands

i'll survey their span

with a compass & ruler

but i'll need not my pan

...

a fucking poem

a fucking poem

fucking thing

with fucking flapping

fucking wings

a fucking bastard

fucking shat

it's fucking this &

fucking that

on fucking death on

fucking love

plus all the other

fucking stuff

that make up fucking

life my friend

a fucking poem

then the end

...

(~)

t
h
e

e
n
d

...

www.ingramcontent.com/pod-product-compliance
Lightning Source LLC
Chambersburg PA
CBHW040834180526

45159CB00001B/189